EXCITING TITLES FROM Scobre EDUCATIONAL

Contemporary Fiction & Sports Adventures

TALES OF THE UNCOOL
6-Book Series

These are the stories of the nerds, geeks, and freaks of Halsey Middle School — and how six self-proclaimed 'uncool' tweens took over their school.

Grades: 4-6
Ages: 8-12   Paperbacks: $8.99
Pages: 64   Library Bound: $27.99

MAGIC LOCKER ADVENTURES
6-Book Series

Three young friends find a magic locker, which takes them back in time. Historic sporting events are in jeopardy unless they right history!

Grades: 3-5
Ages: 8-11   Paperbacks: $8.99
Pages: 48   Library Bound: $27.99

ON THE HARDWOOD 30-Book Series

MVP Books invites readers to stand alongside their favorite NBA superstars *On the Hardwood*. These officially licensed NBA team bios provide an exciting opportunity to learn about where a team has been, and where they are going...

Grades: 4-6
Ages: 8-12   Paperbacks: $8.99
Pages: 48   Library Bound: $27.99

Common Core Aligned   twitter.com/bookbuddymedia   facebook.com/bookbuddymedia

ORDER NOW!

Contact Lerner Publisher Services:
www.LernerBooks.com
Call: 800-328-4929 • **Fax:** 800-332-1132

Lerner
PUBLISHER SERVICES

BY KEVIN SCARPATI

World's Greatest Sporting Events: Indianapolis 500

Scobre Educational
2255 Calle Clara
La Jolla, CA 92037

Scobre Operations & Administration
42982 Osgood Road
Fremont, CA 94539

www.scobre.com
info@scobre.com

Scobre Educational publications may be purchased for
educational, business, or sales promotional use.

Cover and layout design by Jana Ramsay
Edited by Zach Wyner
Copyedited by Renae Reed
Some photos by Newscom

ISBN: 978-1-62920-161-0 (Soft Cover)
ISBN: 978-1-62920-160-3 (Library Bound)
ISBN: 978-1-62920-159-7 (eBook)

INDEX

INTRODUCTION

Roaring engines, lightning fast speeds and thundering crowds can mean only one thing in Indianapolis–it's May and **motorsport** racing is underway. For more than 100 years, the Indianapolis 500-Mile Race has thrilled and captivated fans from across the country and the globe, establishing a reputation as the "Greatest Spectacle in Racing."

The race follows three weeks of grueling competition referred to as the "Month of May," in which drivers put their cars, skills and courage to the test. In the end, the 33 drivers that register the highest speeds earn their place on Indianapolis' famed Motor **Speedway** and the chance to hear those famous words: "Ladies and gentlemen, start your engines!" Once those words are uttered, the 500 hundred mile race in front of more than 300,000 screaming spectators is underway.

Planes leave a vapor trail as they fly over the Indianapolis Motor Speedway prior to the start of the Indianapolis 500.

The unique traditions and rituals that accompany the Indianapolis 500 make this race more than an event–they create a culture. Traditions include camping out on the "Coke Lot," an area near the Coca-Cola plant where spectators set up tents for the weekend; partying in the "Snake Pit," an infield area by Turn 3 where young spectators watch live musical performances; and the "Spectacle of Bands," where numerous marching bands from neighboring high schools entertain early-arriving fans. Perhaps the race's most famous ritual occurs when the Indy 500 winner stands at the finish line and drinks an ice-cold bottle of milk.

Sam Hornish, Jr. pours milk over his face after winning the 90th edition of the Indianapolis 500.

The Indianapolis 500 creates memorable characters, dramatic storylines and, when all is said and done, some very wealthy race car drivers. With cash prizes up to $2.75 million, drivers have more than their legacy at stake. Racing is their livelihood. The Indianapolis 500 gives them the opportunity to become racing legends and provide for their families for generations to come.

A LOOK BACK

The Indianapolis 500 has been making legends and inspiring legions of fans for more than 100 years. However, in the beginning, the creators of this great race had a very humble vision. In 1909, Carl G. Fisher, Arthur C. Newby, James A. Allison and Frank H. Wheeler hatched a plan to build a speedway to test automobiles. With the creation of the "Model T" Ford (America's first mass-produced car), the automobile industry was on the verge of a giant boom. Fisher, Newby, Allison and Wheeler could see that the automobile was here to stay. They believed a speedway on which different cars could be tested would be something in which companies and consumers would both be interested. They could not have known just how right they were. A century later, the Indianapolis 500 is more than a motorsport competition; it is an American **pastime**.

It didn't take long for car testing on the Indianapolis speedway to evolve into car racing. Racing proved to be entertaining and informative, and it rapidly became the Speedway's most popular attraction. Racing offered spectators the chance to watch skilled

The original "Model T" Ford was the first mass-produced automobile in the United States.

drivers compete against one another in the very cars that the spectators could go out and purchase. A huge crowd turnout of more than 15,000 people attended the Speedway's first distance race. Carl G. Fisher called it the 100-lap Prest-O-Lite, naming it after the headlamps that he and James Allison had developed in 1904.

The following year, huge crowds again gathered to see the exciting new paved speedway. Ray Harroun, Joe Dawson, Bob Burman and Barney Oldfield were among the racing stars that competed. Oldfield set a new track mile record in his "Lightning Benz," also known as the "Blitzen Benz." Despite all the excitement, crowds thinned out after the initial races and the rest of the day's events were sparsely attended. The Speedway's owners hatched a new plan. In the hopes of gathering the maximum number of spectators and attracting the country's greatest drivers, they would hold a single race—a demanding 500-mile epic with a large cash prize going to the winner.

The Wheeler-Schebler Trophy, on display at the Indianapolis Motor Speedway Hall of Fame Museum, was first awarded to the winner of the Indianapolis 500 in 1909.

The Alco-6 "Black Beast," on display during "Community Day", ran in the 1911 Indianapolis 500. It had no seat belt and a top speed of 100 mph.

The decision generated huge buzz amongst the press and fans. On Memorial Day weekend, May 30, 1911, the first Indianapolis 500 was held before a massive crowd of 80,000. Forty race car drivers battled it out for fortune and fame and a new tradition was born.

At the first Indy 500, all the drivers had **ride-along mechanics** who would tell the driver when cars were approaching from the rear. All the drivers except for one. Ray Harroun wasn't interested in any help. Having created the first **rearview mirror**, Harroun convinced the race car's owners he could ride alone. In what would be his final race,

Harroun buckled himself into his "Marmon Wasp" and drove solo. He passed the finish line at the head of the pack, won the race and collected $10,000. In the coming years, as interest in the sport exploded, so did the prize money. Today the Indianapolis 500 is the highest paying sporting event in the country.

America's involvement in World War I and World War II each brought racing to a stop for a few years. When the fighting ended, the organizers of the Indy 500 set out to make the race safer. As a result of accident-related deaths, racers were required to wear helmets and safety lights were installed on the track. It was in the post-World War I era that Howdy Wilcox became the first driver to reach speeds of more than 100 miles per hour.

Ray Harroun's "Marmon Wasp," on display at the Children's Museum of Indianapolis.

The "Parade Lap" at the 2014 Indianapolis 500.

Following World War II, the race's popularity surged. While it had already had a presence on the radio, its broadcast on television attracted millions of new fans. In 1961, ABC aired highlights of the Indianapolis 500 as part of its "Wide World of Sports" show. Then, in 1965, they began broadcasting the whole race. 2014 marked the 50th straight year that ABC televised the Indianapolis 500 in its entirety.

Driving lanes are almost always narrow on race day.

TIMELINE

1940
Wilbur Shaw becomes the first driver ever to win the Indy 500 two years in a row. To this day, he remains one of only four drivers to accomplish this feat.

1979
The **pace car** is used for the first time and the "pack up" rule is instated. This means that when the yellow safety light comes on, all cars pack up behind the pace car, giving officials a chance to safely clear debris from a crash.

1900

1925

1950

1975

1916
As World War I intensifies the race is cut to 300 miles to save tires and fuel. Italian-born driver Dario Resta wins the shortened race. After being denied a $5,000 appearance fee, former winner Ralph DePalma refuses to race again.

1931
A record 70 racers compete to participate in the Indy 500. Billy Arnold leads the race until his back **axle** breaks. Tragically, his wheel bounces off the track, crosses a residential street and kills 11-year-old Wilbur C. Brink in the front yard of his house.

1959
Following the deaths of drivers Pat O'Conner, who died when his car flipped over, and Jerry Unser, Jr., who died from severe burns, two new rules are adopted. All cars are required to install **roll-over bars** and all racers are required to wear fireproof suits.

1911
Forty cars compete in the first-ever Indy 500—then called the "International Sweepstakes." With an average speed of 74.6 mph, Ray Harroun is the race's first winner. He is the first driver to use a rearview mirror.

SPEED LIMIT 75

1975
A multi-million dollar museum is built to increase appreciation of the beloved sport. Attendees can now view 75 classic automobiles, racing cars and motorcycles. The site is later listed in the National Register of Historic Places.

2014
To increase competition, the Indy 500 announces changes to the qualifying format. Racers will now have two on-track days to determine their starting position. On Day Two, the top nine qualifiers will participate in a "Fast Nine Shootout" to determine the **pole position** winner.

1999
In the race's 83rd year, Kenny Brack becomes the Indy 500 champion. During the race, the Indianapolis Motor Speedway hosts a number of Congressional Medal of Honor recipients to mark the Speedway's 90th anniversary.

1985   1995   2005   2015

1986
Improvements in design and technology help Bobby Rahal became the first race car driver to complete the 500-mile race in less than three hours.

2006
Sam Hornish, Jr. makes Indy 500 history with the closest win in the history of the event. He surges past rookie Marco Andretti at the finish line, winning the trophy by 0.063 seconds

THE FUTURE

As the Indianapolis 500 has grown in popularity and speeds have climbed, race car drivers have become some of the world's most beloved athletes. New technologies allow these masterful drivers to register speeds once thought unreachable. Besides falling records, another thing to watch for in the future is the trend of crossover drivers who race in the Indy 500, Brickyard 400 and United States Grand Prix. With fame and fortune on the line, more and more drivers will be eager to start their engines and race their way into the history books.

EQUIPMENT

The most important piece of equipment at the Indy 500 is no mystery—it's the car. Indy 500 cars are state-of-the-art and extremely expensive. Technological breakthroughs have paved the way for **turbocharged** engines with direct **fuel injection** and the ability to produce more **horsepower** with lighter equipment.

The **anatomy** of an Indy car consists of 29 top-of-the-line parts. These parts include everything from the oil scavenge tower, brake master cylinder and engine control unit, to the molded seat and impact lights. The chassis is known as the car's "spine." It includes the driver's compartment, fuel vent and roll hoop. The chassis is what makes it possible for the driver to control the car.

Fuel-injected **V6 engines** help the racers accelerate with ease, while the side pod—which covers important areas of the car such as the water radiator—helps the engine stay cool and makes the cars more aerodynamic. Turbocharged engines harness 550 to 700 horsepower.

A driver's helmet is a complex piece of equipment that provides protection from debris, air resistance and heat. The outer shell distributes energy during impact, and the Nomex lining absorbs sweat and relocates heat. In addition to the

Equipment plays a large role in driver safety.

helmet, other safety gear has improved to keep drivers cool. The Nomex fire suit is made of fire-resistant material that is designed to protect the drivers from direct flames and second- or third-degree burns.

All of these advances have made it possible for drivers to push themselves and their cars to the limit. As technology continues to leap forward, drivers and their fans will continue to reap the benefits in the form of faster speeds and safer conditions.

VENUE

INDIANAPOLIS MOTOR SPEEDWAY

Entrance to the Indianapolis Motor Speedway in Speedway, Indiana.

"Speedway" is more than the name of the Indy 500 track. It is also a town located in Marion County, Indiana, and it has been the permanent home of the Indy 500 since the race's beginning in 1909.

The track for which Speedway, Indiana was named.

The Indianapolis Motor Speedway (IMS) track was originally built to give car companies a place to test different models before they were sold to the public. When the Speedway's owners recognized the potential for commercial success in a single, epic race, they created the "Greatest Spectacle in Racing." Since then, the IMS has been the home of several motorsport races including the Red Bull Indianapolis GP, the Brickyard 400 and the United States Grad Prix.

Tens of thousands of racing fans from across the country travel to Speedway, Indiana every Memorial Day weekend, but the motor-tourism doesn't stop during the offseason. Even when there are no races being run, fans come for a ground tour of the Speedway, for a chance to see the venue in a way that would be impossible during racing season. In these quieter months, visitors can get up close and personal with the famed "Yard of Bricks," stroll the Pagoda and even take a ride around the 2.5-mile track. In addition, the IMS Hall of Fame Museum offers fans a stroll down memory lane, with photographs and mementos from the most memorable moments in the Indy 500's storied history.

RULES

Being a fast driver isn't the only thing racers need to concern themselves with. Like any other sport, the Indy 500 is governed by a strict set of rules and regulations. Rules focus on everything from the inspection of individual vehicles and qualifying for the race. Other guidelines include pit stops and rules of the racing road.

As of 2014, Indy 500 racers now have two days of time trials to obtain the top spots in the race. For some, Day One times will be erased on Day Two, giving drivers in the 10th to 33rd spot the chance to make up for a subpar day. Also on Day Two, the top nine cars compete in an intense, heart-stopping four-lap race for pole position known as the "Fast Nine Shootout."

With cars blazing along at speeds of more than 220 mph, safety is a huge priority—especially given the race's history of devastating accidents. Rules requiring safe conditions for drivers include mandatory fire suits as well as the addition of roll-over bars. Before the race,

An Indy race car in action.

Team Pennzoil makes a pit stop early on in the 2014 Indy 500.

officials inspect driver's cars to make sure their engines meet proper specifications. No illegal boosting of the engines is allowed.

During the race, cars pull off the track to refuel and get new tires. This is called a "pit stop." There are numerous rules that state how many mechanics can work on the cars and what techniques they may use in order to get their car back on the track as quickly as possible. Amazingly, the average pit stop time at the Indy 500 is 10-14 seconds.

THE ROAD TO...

The long road to the IMS takes many shapes and forms, often beginning under the humblest of circumstances. Many winners of the Borg-Warner Trophy ("Baby Borg") got their start behind the wheel of a go-kart. But however they got started, every single driver who has taken the wheel behind a state-of-the-art race car and competed for pole position at the Indy 500 has something in common. They have all made huge investments of money, energy and time in their racing car and career.

The most common thread in the stories of all IndyCar race car drivers has been the pressing need to drive really fast. Those compelled to follow this desire, and eager to experience the world of open-wheeled cars, can compete in several racing series in order to work their way up to the "Greatest Spectacle in Racing."

One popular path that young drivers take is the Mazda Road to Indy. This system allows drivers to familiarize themselves with race cars that have the same tires and chassis as those race cars used in the Indy 500. In their training, these young race car drivers experience all three IndyCar disciplines: oval, road and street circuit courses. The Mazda Road has become a true test to see if drivers can handle the oval track at the IMS.

Go-karts are a common step on the road to race car driving.

Race car drivers must get accustomed to oval tracks if they want to excel on the Indianapolis Motor Speedway.

BEST PERFORMANCES

SAM HORNISH, JR., 2006

In 2006, it appeared that reigning Indy 500 champ Dan Wheldon had the 90th Indy 500 all wrapped up. Leading for 148 laps, Whedon's car got a flat tire and was instantly sidelined for repairs. Whedon was able to get back into the mix, but his stranglehold on the race was broken. Amazing the spectators, Sam Hornish, Jr. came from behind to take the lead in the final lap. When rookie Marco Andretti edged ahead of him on his right side, Hornish, Jr. showed the skill that had earned him the pole position and the determination of a champion who would not be denied. In the final stretch, he surged ahead of Andretti, winning the race by a mere 0.0635 seconds, taking home his first Baby Borg trophy, and becoming the first Indy 500 winner in the race's long history to overtake a leader on the final lap.

TOMMY MILTON, 1921 & 1923

The gritty early years of the Indy 500 had men racing without fire suits and helmets. This fact didn't stop hundreds of race car drivers from putting rubber to the road. One such brave man was Tommy Milton. Driving with impaired vision (a condition that would eliminate him from today's competition), Milton won the race twice. His first victory came in 1921. The following year, thousands of fans cheered him on, hoping he might repeat the feat. However, fuel problems sidelined him for remainder of the race after just 44 laps.

The focus and energy Milton poured into the 1923 Indy 500 took its toll. Battling foot cramps after the first 100 laps, blisters broke out on his hands from gripping the steering wheel so hard. Needing immediate medical attention, Milton sidelined his car and Howdy Wilcox stepped in as his relief driver for laps 103 through 151. This gave Milton all the time he needed to recover and refocus. After lap 151, he retook the wheel from Wilcox and won the race, becoming the first two-time winner in Indy 500 history.

A.J. FOYT, 1977

In 1977, seasoned veteran A.J. Foyt took the track in search of a record fourth Indy 500 win. It had been 10 years since he had taken home the Baby Borg trophy, but he was confident he had another win in him. During the race, scorching heat knocked out nearly half the field, leaving only 17 cars in the running. Just two laps after taking a small lead, Foyt had to pit to refuel and get his right side tires fixed. He fell 32 seconds behind leader Gordon Jonhcock. Knowing he needed to make up time fast, Foyt risked his engine's life, turning up his turbo boost. The risk paid off. Foyt made up nearly two seconds per lap and then took the lead for good when Johncock's engine expired. Foyt took home his fourth Baby Borg trophy and wrote himself into the record books.

DAN WHELDON, 2005

Dan Wheldon is known for saying "I put everything into my racing." In the 2005 Indianapolis 500, "everything" propelled him to a dramatic victory. In a banner year for the Indianapolis 500, rookie driver Danica Patrick became the first woman in the history of the race to lead laps. Following a back-and-forth battle, with 10 laps to go Patrick darted around Wheldon and held the lead for three laps. Wheldon responded, flooring his accelerator, roaring past Patrick, and holding his lead for the final seven heart-stopping laps. Not bothered by a competitor's crash, Wheldon crossed the finish line under the yellow and white caution flag and became the first British driver to win the Indy 500 since Graham Hill back in 1966.

THE RECORD BOOK

In the more than 100-year history of the Indy 500, three drivers have won the race four times: A.J. Foyt, Al Unser, Jr. and Rick Mears.

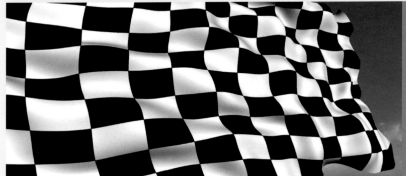

At the young age of 22 years, two months and 19 days, Troy Ruttman became the youngest winner of the Indy 500 back in 1952—a record that has stood for more than 60 years.

With four Indy 500 wins in 11 races, driver Al Unser is the all-time lap leader. Over the span of his career, Unser, Jr. was utterly dominant, leading for a total of 644 laps.

Johnny Rutherford and Al Unser went nose-to-nose in the 1970 qualifier. Unser crossed the finish line one hundredth (.01) of a second ahead of Rutherford.

Flying around the oval track at 222.574 mph, Emerson Fittipaldi set the record for the fastest lap at 40.436 seconds.

In 2014, three-time Indy 500 winner Helio Castroneves finished the full 500-mile race for a record 10th time.

THE FANS

Fans of the Indianapolis 500 are among the most passionate in all of sports.

Ever since the IMS first opened to the public, crowds have flocked en masse to see state-of-the-art cars driven by the best race car drivers in the country. In 1911, a spectacular 60,000-person crowd assembled to watch the first Indy 500. Today, crowds have swelled to five times that number. In 2013, more than 300,000 people attended the "Greatest Spectacle in Racing." Such massive turnouts have made it the largest spectator sport in the country. In addition to those in attendance, millions of fans from across the globe tune in to watch the race live on television.

Fans take in the action at the 2001 Indy 500.

The road to becoming the largest spectator sport in the country has been one filled with innovation. In order to attract more fans, the Indy 500 designed areas specifically geared to entertain fans of varied ages. For the more youthful fans, the Kids Zone provides music, games and prizes. Meanwhile, adults looking to rock out to live music party down in the Snake Pit. Whatever their age, operators of the Indy 500 try to ensure that every racing fan gets a seat. Seating prices start at a reasonable $40 with penthouse tickets priced closer to $200.

The Indy 500 provides one of the greatest fan experiences in all sports. Fans can closely monitor the race, play games and party all day. Whether or not their favorite driver wins, fans walk away from the race fully satisfied, counting the days until the next Memorial Day.

IMPACT

The IMS and the sport of auto racing had humble beginnings. However, when the decision was made to hold one big race, the Indy 500 roared onto the national stage and became a significant part of the American sports landscape. For more than a century, the race has grown every year, becoming more and more competitive and gaining an international audience.

Each year, the end of May means a national spotlight for Speedway, Indiana, as thousands of people flock to the Midwest. During this time, the local economy receives a huge boost with revenue in excess of $500 million. The boost benefits both the local businesses and the drivers, with the race's top finishers sharing more than $14 million in prize money.

When all is said and done, one driver's dreams are realized. After 500 miles, only one driver stands alone atop the podium, the recipient of the Borg-Warner Trophy. But the credit for making this race the great event it is today does not go solely to the winner. Every single driver, crewmember and fan that travels to Speedway, Indiana deserves recognition for their loyalty and dedication. "The Greatest Spectacle in Racing," with its continual advancements and its community of millions, is a testament to the passion of its founders, as well as the participants and fans that carry on the

Helio Castroneves hugs the Borg-Warner Trophy after winning his second-straight Indy 500.

Glossary

anatomy: a study of the structure or internal workings of something.

axle: a rod or spindle (either fixed or rotating) passing through the center of a wheel or group of wheels.

fuel injection: an internal-combustion engine that delivers fuel or a fuel-air mixture to the cylinders by means of pressure from a pump.

horsepower: the power that a horse exerts in pulling.

motorsport: a sport involving the racing of motor vehicles, especially cars and motorcycles.

pace car: a car that sets the pace and positions racers for a rolling start in a warm-up lap or laps before a race, or that returns to control the pace in temporarily hazardous conditions.

pastime: an activity that someone does regularly for enjoyment rather than work.

pole position: the most favorable position at the start of an automobile race, typically on the inside of the front row of competitors.

rearview mirror: a small angled mirror fixed inside the windshield of a motor vehicle, enabling the driver to see the vehicle or road behind.

ride-along mechanic: a mechanic that rode along with a race car during races, and who was tasked with maintaining, monitoring and repairing the car during the race. They also communicated with the pits and spotted from inside the car.

roll-over bars: bars installed to prevent injury in the case of an accident in which the race car rolls over.

speedway: a stadium or track used for automobile or motorcycle racing.

turbocharger: a device that supplies air to an engine at a higher pressure than normal to increase the engine's power.

V6 engine: a "V" engine with six cylinders mounted on the crankcase in two banks of three cylinders,